Imagine ME...

Conquering Fears, Stigmas and Regrets

"Yet in all these things we are more than conquerors through Him who loved us" Romans 8:37 (NKJV)

Sistar' Warrior,
    Lethar,

Arise in your greatness & WAR
for your bloodline!

AYoungLady

Contents

Dedication

To my Lord and Savior Jesus Christ, the Author and Finisher of my faith, and of this book you hold. The inspiration of this book; the instructions, thoughts, ideas, graphics, etc. are all Holy Spirit inspired, solely. I'll dedicate this book to no other than the Source of why and how it came into fruition. This book has been rightfully submitted unto the only wise God for Kingdom impact. All honor, all power, all glory belongs to El Elyon, God most high!

"To God our Savior, Who alone is wise, Be glory and majesty, Dominion and power, Both now and forever. Amen." Jude 1:25 (NKJV)

Acknowledgements

To my sexy man of God, my king, and loving husband, Mr. Ray Young. Thank you for your support and accountability in completing this project. Thank you for loving me so much. I love, honor, respect and adore your headship in my life as unto our God. Your patience with me is impeccable. Truly, being married to you has matured me in so many ways. I'm definitely not who I used to be, for being married to you has placed a demand on the grown woman you see manifesting before your very eyes today. Outside of God, you're everything to me. You're beautifully AMAZING! Forever in love with You (German Chocolate)!!!

To my parents, Pearl & Liston Smith, Jr. I honor you both, as unto the Lord; that my days will be long on this earth. I continue to live for and serve the God you both introduced me to. Your prayers, how you raised me, your years of sacrifice and labor for the baby girl entrusted to you both, were not in vain. May God bless and overflow you both with rewards that surpass your comprehension; for your spiritual upbringing and investment in me. I love, honor and respect you both.

To my spiritual parents, Bishop John & Pastor Isha Edmondson. Thank you for the

life changing Word taught in simplicity.
Thank you for speaking life into me, and for
always declaring the Anointing on my life.
Thank you for being 'responsible shepherds'
of your flock and doing your very best to
reflect the love of God with each rebuke,
chastisement, and correction. Thank you
both for teaching your flock that we are
just as anointed and appointed power houses
of God as you both are; that you just
happen to have the microphone. I love you
both to life.

To the Mentors, Life Coaches & Therapists
that have journeyed with me: Assata Michelle
Thomas, Shannon White, Angela Clack. Thank
you all for your services rendered. So very
necessary and rewarding. All my notes,
every session and every nugget taught, are
forever precious and will never lose value.
You ladies helped to resuscitate the anointed
woman of God I am today. I'm so glad I made
the choice to receive the help I desperately
needed. And, I'm super proud of my mental
and emotional health journey to wellness and
wholeness. Grateful to you ladies.

To my 'real, divinely appointed friends' who've
shared in my 'growing pains'. You've held onto
me, even when you didn't want to. You saw
the bigger picture; you saw a better me on
the horizon. You've poured into me, prayed

and declared over me. **You know who each of you are.** Thank you for never letting go, for never turning your backs, for never giving up. It's safe to assume where God's taking you, based on who He connects you to. I love you ladies to life.

To my Creative Writing Coach of RWS, LLC, Giselle Ogando. You've been nothing short of amazing from day one. Thank you for your encouragement and your overwhelming, unexpected excitement for the journey of this project. Clearly, I wasn't just another client for you. Thank you for being led by the Holy Spirit on how to assist me in bringing this necessary reading tool to life. Your sweet spirit and accountability made the process easier than I ever anticipated. Thank you, thank you, thank you.

Forward

"But the Helper (Comforter, Advocate, Intercessor-Counselor, Strengthener, Standby), the Holy Spirit, whom the Father will send in My name [in My place, to represent Me and act on My behalf], He will teach you all things. And He will help you remember everything that I have told you."
John 14:26 (AMP)

"Now then go, and I, even I, will be with your mouth, and will teach you what you shall say."
Exodus 4:12 (AMP)

Preface

The title of this book was birthed out of a connection with the single 'Imagine Me' by gospel recording artist Kirk Franklin from his 2005 album, *Hero*. I connect with this song each time I hear it. This song continually ministers to, continually heals and continually restores the little girl within me. Yet, it wasn't until 2014 that I would hasten to the voice of God to step out on faith and begin writing this book.

Imagine ME...is a two-fold book title.

<u>To my inner self</u>: It's the never-ending, imperfect, progressive journey of a humbled, yet, confidently bold and fierce woman of God encouraging herself, like David did, in the things of God. I choose to stand bold and confident in God's Word amidst the lies, whispers, and suggestions of the enemy. On the canvas of my imagination, I've **dared to imagine** a better me, a transparent me, an unashamed me, an imperfect-progressive me, made possible only through the powerful, cleansing blood of Christ Jesus.

<u>To my readers</u>: The woman you may know; the woman you've encountered; the woman with whom you may be on some level of relationship; the woman you see put together

more times than not, her face beat with makeup on a regular, dark blue hair and close trimmed edges lined up and on point, nails 'did and done', serving and dedicated in ministry, successfully married and loving' it; that woman. Now, imagine the unseen and unnoticeable struggles, the torments of this woman, who once upon a time hid behind a pretty and sophisticated mask. Would you have ever guessed it, or put two and two together? Unless you have spiritual discernment in the Holy Spirit, the way I look outwardly belies what I've dealt with inwardly.

But I no longer live in the bondage of having it all together. I no longer wear the mask of perfection. I have come to terms with the generational bloodline curses I've allowed to burden and consume my life for far too long; and it stops with ME!

The interesting truth is, as an author, by no means have I 'arrived'. I continue to be on the potter's wheel being molded, forgiven, graced, pardoned, and made new daily. Please make no mistake about it, I have not written this book as a means to rid myself of the issues I've faced. Rather, I'm still going through the "process," which is the continual, daily purging of these issues I will later discuss in this book.

The enemy of my mind, heart and emotions waits me out every day, angry that I awake every morning because he fears I'll triumph yet another day in victory through Christ Jesus. And he's never been more right! I'm determined to make it to the finish line. I've come too far to turn back. Some days can be challenging, however that's expected as the enemy stays on his job; and I'm on my job. I'm looking for the enemy to pick a fight with him because I'm sure to win, only because of WHO I belong to. **I John 4:4** says greater is He that is within me, than he that is in the world. And, according to **Isaiah 54:17**, no weapon that is formed against me will prosper.

NOW! It's payback time against the enemy! The appointed time to share with the nations my story of God's continual love and saving grace toward me, in spite of me, and to encourage other men and women to step out on faith and share their testimonies of the saving grace of the almighty God.

As you read this material, I'm certain you will be able to relate to the same, if not similar struggles and torments within your life, currently or previously. Be encouraged and empowered to ***imagine yourself*** more than a conqueror over fears, stigma and regrets.

"Yet in all these things we are more than conquerors through Him who loved us"
Romans 8:37 (NKJV)

WE WIN!!!

Conquering Fears

"For God has not given us a spirit of fear, but of power and of love and of a sound mind."

2 Timothy 1:7 (NKJV)

Fear as defined by Dictionary.com, is a distressing emotion aroused by impending danger, evil, pain, etc., whether the threat is real or imagined; the feeling or condition of being afraid.

From what I've perceived to be lurking in a dark room to the failure and success of a business, to the negative opinions and the rejection of others; I've allowed the spirit of F.E.A.R. (also known as: FALSE EVIDENCE APPEARING REAL) to grip my imagination, heart, and emotions. From adolescence to adulthood, the spirit of fear has walked with me, talked to me, even seemed comforting - which is completely a trick of the enemy!

That part, the spirit of fear seemingly a comforter? Fear is a deceiver. I dealt with fear incorrectly. I gave in to it and did myself a disservice. I accepted fear as my day-to-day life. I became uncomfortably comfortable with the dysfunction of the spirit of fear. Now, how's that for

12

confusion? I accepted fear as a normality in my conscious mind, although I was fully aware of its abnormality in my subconscious mind. I just sat in it and gave up on being freed of it. I made do. Sadly, I seemingly made peace with the spirit of fear, which is a perverted combination and utter deception. **For God has not given us a spirit of fear, but of power and of love and of a sound mind. 2 Timothy 1:7 (NKJV).**

I hoped fear would someday, somehow, unbeknownst to me, just evaporate without any effort on my part. And, when fear didn't disappear or wear off as I had expected, I accepted fear, the same way I accepted my nasal allergies. Fear, like my allergies, are hereditary for me, therefore I must live with it, right?

WRONG!

So, what was the underlying issue? Why was it so difficult for me to evict the spirit of fear from my life? Fear hangs with a few buddies that tag along and carry their own demonic assignments. For example, the spirit of torment is besties with fear! **There is no fear in love; but perfect love casts out fear, because fear involves torment. But he who fears has not been made perfect in love, 1 John 4:18 (NKJV).** I was unwilling to put in the necessary work to obtain and maintain my deliverance, even though I wanted to be free of the spirit of fear, and I wanted the positive outcome of freedom.

The work is a serious commitment. It's not for the faint of heart or spiritual punks. It's warfare at its finest! You've got to put on the full armor of God, **Ephesians 6:13-17**, get into warfare mode, and remain until you've experienced your breakthrough! **"For the weapons of our warfare are not carnal but mighty in God for the pulling down strongholds" 2 Corinthians 10:4 (NKJV).**

The two main weapons mighty through God to pull down the stronghold of the spirit of fear are 1. praying (declaring out loud) scriptures on fear and 2. your faith. You've got to boldly maneuver through whatever, whenever, despite your fickle feelings. Do not trust how you feel, they are temporary! Move in faith of God's Word.

"Even though I walk through the [sunless] valley of the shadow of death, I fear no evil, for You are with me; Your rod [to protect] and Your staff [to guide], they comfort and console me." Psalm 23:4 (AMP).

Keep moving, keep applying for jobs, keep applying to schools, keep serving at church! Stay your course in that dreadful marriage (it gets better!). Keep trying to have that baby, keep writing that book, start that business, keep declaring God's Word, keep loving those difficult children, keep walking boldly through or past those dark corners of your home, keep warring in the spirit of Christ. Whatever you do, keep moving! That's your faith in action. That is your corresponding, suitable, appropriate action! Remember, God said it in His Word, He's with you to console and comfort you.

Even during the journey of writing this book, I had to come to terms with the spirit of intimidation (which is a manifestation of fear and torment, I John 4:18) due to a lack of a college degree; that's been deeply rooted for years. I've come across a hand full of people with college degrees (in and outside of my bloodline unit) that I allowed to make me feel less than intelligent because I dropped out of college. The enemy often whispered the lies that I am not intelligent, that I have nothing to offer anyone, that no one would listen to me because I sound uneducated. From one-on-one or group-setting conversations, to presentations, or leading prayer at church; I've been intimidated in too many instances to open my mouth. Many times, I've kept quiet out of fear that I would say something that made no sense to anyone, that I would sound discombobulated. BUT THE DEVIL IS A SAD LIAR!!!

When you begin to search through God's Word on your specific situation, revelation breeds transformation. This next scripture gave me a whole new outlook on how to deal with the spirit of fear. **"Have I not commanded you? Be strong and courageous! Do not be terrified or dismayed (intimidated), for the Lord your God is with you wherever you go." Joshua 1:9 (AMP)**

Now, don't misunderstand, we serve a loving and merciful God, full of grace. He has already provided everything we need to be victorious in Him!! Which is why the first five words of that scripture says, **"Have I not commanded you?"** So, wait; you mean discarding the spirits of fear, terror, dismay and intimidation out of my life is an order? A command? A demand? **YES!**

It's not even up for discussion. And, it's no wonder; with all the tools God has provided us to separate ourselves from the spirit of fear, it's a command - period! Upon my revelation of this scripture, transformation was inevitable. Walking in the spirit of fear another day was unacceptable. Entertaining night terror (even in the daylight) is now unacceptable. Entertaining fear of success, fear of failure, fear of the negative opinions and rejections of others, and even fear of the dark is now unacceptable. When you acquire a greater knowledge of the Word of God, you are now held accountable, and therefore required to perform at a greater level. **Much is required from those to whom much is given, for their responsibility is greater. Luke 12:48,b (TLB).** There was no longer an excuse for me to perish in the spirit of fear, for I no longer lacked the knowledge thereof. According to the repercussions of **Hosea 4:6**, if you reject knowledge, then God will reject you. I don't recommend rejecting God's knowledge.

God gave us the spirit of HIS power, HIS love, and HIS sound mind; all precious commodities! The part of the scripture in **Joshua 1:9** where it says, **'Do not be,'** our God is saying, don't be discouraged about the instructions He gives us, but to stand on what He has said. For, if we truly believe the Word of God, meditating and practicing God's Word, then we won't allow the enemy, nor our adversaries punk us or rule us. And, God commands this strength and boldness of us!

For the weapons of our warfare are not carnal but mighty in God for pulling down strongholds. 2 Corinthians 10:4 (NKJV)

Death and life are in the power of the tongue. Proverbs 18:21 (NKJV)

And be renewed in the spirit of your mind. Ephesians 4:23 (NKJV)

God has commanded us to separate from the spirit of fear. As you can see from the above scriptures, God has given us the tools necessary to remain forever separated from fear's torment. It's that simple - all glory be to God!

"The Lord *is* my light and my salvation; Whom shall I fear? The Lord *is* the strength of my life; Of whom shall I be afraid?" Psalm 27:1 (NKJV)

Conquering Stigmas

"I've told you these things to prepare you for rough times ahead. They are going to throw you out of the meeting places. There will even come a time when anyone who kills you will think he's doing God a favor. They will do these things because they never really understood the Father. I've told you these things so that when the time comes and they start in on you, you'll be well-warned and ready for them."

John 16:1-4 (MSG)

Stigma as defined in the Cambridge English Dictionary, is a strong lack of respect for a person or a group of people; or a bad opinion of them because they have done something society does not approve of.

All too often, when a person is labelled by their behavior, they are no longer seen as an individual, but as part of a stereotype. As a result, negative attitudes and beliefs can create prejudice which leads to negative actions and discrimination.

From a few relatives, to church leaders and former friends; I've dealt with the stigma of being the person that others (sadly even myself, having believed the opinions of others) have negatively declared me to be far too long. I'm now able to distinguish the difference between the old me (my generational bloodline) and the anointed child of God that I am. PRAISE GOD!

In order for me to be assured of the difference between the stigma and the anointing I walk in, I must continually rehearse scripture, and I must believe and know I am the righteousness of God in Christ Jesus. Present day, the enemy continues to work overtime to have me think I haven't changed, or matured in God at at all.

On the contrary!

God continually ministers to my heart and confirms; therefore, because I have changed, grown and matured, I'm now eligible to encounter new levels of warfare. Because I've graduated to the next level (have not arrived nor am I perfect) I'm equipped and now able to crush, dismantle, and destroy the works of the enemy!

The new devils or new circumstances you face are not necessarily attributed to you having done anything wrong. However, a variety of times we willingly make wrong choices which are now wrong in its entirety, and therefore causes wrong circumstances and consequences. However, it's important to remember your fight is never against flesh and blood (people). **"For we do not wrestle against flesh and blood, but against principalities, against powers, against the rulers of the darkness of this age, against spiritual** *hosts* **of wickedness in the heavenly** *places*." Ephesians 6:12 (NKJV)

You and I have a common, unseen enemy who will try to play us against each other and implode the harmony of our units at work, church, and in our bloodlines, if we allow him. The more you hunger, thirst, and chase hard after the things of God, the more the enemy chases after you, to distract you with anything and anyone. **"The thief does not come except to steal, and to kill, and to destroy. I have come that they may have life, and that they may have** *it* **more abundantly."** John 10:10 (NKJV)

November of 2015 was significant in that it was one of many instances in which God manifested His Word in my life, found in **Psalm 23:5a (AMP) "You prepare a table before me in the presence of my enemies."** I've actually witnessed God prepare a table before me in the very presence of known enemies! In other words, I've experienced God's provision of vindication and vengeance for me in the midst of an all out attack. When God brings you through to the other side of opposition, He won't do it in private, He will do it openly for all your enemies to see!! Which is why we don't have to take it upon ourselves to avenge ourselves. David makes mention in **Psalm 23:5** that God has prepared him a banquet in the presence of his enemies, who had to stand back and watch as he basked in the favor of the Lord, and they can't do anything about it. That God prepares David a banquet table in front of his enemies, is the ultimate rebuke of them. Now how's that for God's power!! Notice, David never went up against his main enemy, Saul. David never took upon himself to avenge himself.

God wastes nothing - not even your enemies!

God will often use your enemy to establish your identity in Christ by way of opposition. Often, God will allow and use for good what the enemy brings to keep you stirred up and hungry for the things of God. He'll allow this to keep you focused and determined to go after what they said you couldn't do or become; and, only for the manifested truth to be to the glory of God!! God will use your enemies and critics to bless you! Oppositions are not meant to stop you, rather to catapult you to your destiny and push you forward. The work of your enemies may look like a setback, but it's a set-up for your ultimate success. **When the** enemy comes in like a flood, the Spirit of the Lord will lift up a standard against him. Isaiah 59:19 (NKJV)

'There's a cost for 'Wellness.' Sometimes people talking about you and judging you is the price. YOU are responsible for your wellness. How bad do you want it?"

~Assata Michelle Thomas, Spiritual Life Coach

It's important for you to remember the last situation God brought you through triumphantly. Recall the last table (God's vindication/vengeance on your behalf) that was prepared just for you in the presence of your enemies and encourage yourself when faced with your next enemy, which is sure to come. When facing your enemy, don't back down and don't lose heart, no matter how seemingly intimidating. Do as God instructs; and you're sure to win every time! **"Moreover David said, 'The Lord, who delivered me from the paw of the lion and from the paw of the bear, He will deliver me from the hand of this Philistine.'" I Samuel 17:37 (NKJV)**

In no way have I been perfect. I've sown my share of offenses throughout my life. I've received clear revelation from God that though I must obey His Word, repent, and ask forgiveness of God and those whom I've offended, I need not go any further. I need not render any explanation for my imperfections, because we all are equally imperfect. We all were born into sin, shaped into iniquity from the womb **(Psalm 51:5)** And, for those of us who have accepted Christ's sacrifice on the cross, we are a part of one body, the body of Christ; making us equally righteous **(2 Corinthians 5:21).**

We all have diverse categories of imperfections, but not any that are more or less than that of our neighbor; not to be confused in any way. The enemy really tried to convince me that my shortcomings were so increasingly different or intense than that of others. What a complete lie!! The Word of God clearly reveals that we are equally imperfect, regardless of whether we commit the same offenses or not. We all were born in sin and iniquity equally. We all, having accepted Christ as Lord and Savior, are made righteous through Christ Jesus equally. The prerequisite for becoming cleansed through the blood of Christ is the same for us all.

Therefore, there's no such thing as a major sin verses a minor sin, a big sin or little sin. My wrong is just as wrong as the next wrong of my brothers and sisters in Christ, and of those who are not born again. We all must be careful not to judge another person's shortcomings just because it may not be our particular shortcoming. Let's be careful not to look down or disassociate ourselves with those whose struggles are not our own. **I Corinthians 5:10.**

When we really look at this from God's perspective, He doesn't see murder as a bigger sin than a lie. God doesn't see stealing any smaller than gossip. God sees it all as sin, period. To label or place stigmas on our fellow brothers and sisters obviously does not please God (**I John 4:8, Matthew 6:15**), and is undoubtedly hurtful to that individual. We must practice building each other up. **"Do not let unwholesome [foul, profane, worthless, vulgar] words ever come out of your mouth, but only such speech as is good for building up others, according to the need and the occasion, so that it will be a blessing to those who hear [you speak]." Ephesians 4:29 (AMP)**

"Don't let negative treatment from others toward you be the expression of your Heavenly Father."

~Bishop John Edmondson, Victory in Christ Christian Center

I've had to let this teaching from my spiritual father sink in deeply in my mind and burn

25

away years of "stinkin' thinkin'." In times past because of my spiritual immaturity, I was in a place in my life where I thought that, if someone particularly in church leadership rendered me negative or unfair treatment, then it must be how God feels toward me as well. I really believed, since church leaders were seemingly anointed, operating in the Holy Spirit, still speaking in tongues, still prophesying, still laying hands and actually being effective; then the God in them must be just as angry with me and just as disappointed with me. I assumed God must be sick and tired of me to the same degree that my church leaders negatively treated me.

What an absolute lie I discovered this to be!! And then I was reminded of this scripture, **"For the gifts and the calling of God are irrevocable [for He does not withdraw what He has given, nor does He change His mind about those to whom He gives His grace or to whom He sends His call]." Romans 11:29 (AMP).**

So you see, from church leaders to congregants, the gifts and callings of God on one's life are under full warranty-never canceled and never rescinded. Even while you are yet in sin, yet hurtful to others; you are still able to be used by God. Not to be confused in any way with God approving the hurt imposed by those He still uses for His Kingdom. Please understand, no one is perfect...in or outside of the church, saved or unsaved. However, God is love and He doesn't approve of anyone hurting another, and we all will be held accountable by Him.

(Thankfully, none of the following experiences have occurred present day)

In times passed, I've experienced being one of many women wrongfully ostracized as a homewrecker, and accused of being secretly involved with a pastor.

I've been in situations where leadership wrongfully assumed the worst about me, and failed to handle me appropriately, (having not operated in God's love). I've been unfairly judged and presupposed by former leadership without the opportunity for a dialog, regarding what the root of my issues really were.

Inspite of being given the responsibility by God to build up their congregants; I've been on the receiving end of judgemental, non-loving, harsh words from previous leadership, who declared what they'd perceived me to be, rather than declaring what God' Word says I am. Instead, I was torn down, and key details about my personal struggles, situations and even assumptions and misconceptions were exposed publicly.

The stigma given to me by former leadership resulted in the idea that maybe my church membership should be terminated, and I be banned from attending that church all together.

I've experienced rejection and negative treatment from others as if my 'issues' were a contagious illness, in an attempt to follow suite with the stigma previous leadership had placed on me. Much later, even with the attempt to publicly remove the reproach placed on me; unbeknownst to this leader, major mental and emotional damage had already taken root within me. Thank God for Jesus; *the only One* capable of removing reproach from one's life. **"...he will love you and not accuse you...I have gathered your wounded and taken away your reproach." Zephaniah 3:17b-18 (TLB)**

As you can see, I've experienced deep hurt and pain, which resulted in years of mental and emotional bondage due to stigmas. However, I had to decide whether or not I was going to let those hurtful experiences be my future. As time has passed, I realized whether or not these former church leaders, former friends and acquaintances have acknowledged their negative treatment toward me is out of my control, and has only made me better; because now I've received revelation on God's truth regarding my identity in Christ!! All glory and praise to God for a renewed mind in Christ Jesus! **(Ephesians 4:23).**

Here's a sad truth

It's utterly offensive to some people that you no longer resemble 'THAT THING' which they've stigmatized you as because of Jesus' powerful cleansing blood! (In some cases, you never were that stigma to begin with). Some people don't like the fact that you can be free of your 'old, sinful-man' without their permission. Some people want to watch you suffer, spiritually die, and memorialize who you were; what you did; and what you said. They don't want to give you grace. Unfortunately for some, the stigma they've given you is a necessary conversation piece, which allows them to deflect their own imperfections and shortcomings..

I'll let you absorb that for a moment.

Here's a joyful truth

No matter what people do against us, God will always use it for our good, to our benefit. **Genesis 50:20.**

I'm in a place where some people don't have the capacity to withhold who I'm called to be, BECAUSE NOW...I'm so much stronger and wiser; I'm still standing, having risen in the power, strength, anointing and favor of God on my successful, imperfect journey to my destiny!!!

That settles the matter of being labeled, stigmatized and ostracized for they truly help us become all were created to be in Christ Jesus. Be encouraged people of God and go forth! Tell your haters and your naysayers, "THANKS Y'ALL!!!" It's all good. To God be the glory for the things HE has done!

"Let my verdict of vindication come from Your presence; May Your eyes look with equity and behold things that are just." Psalm 17:2 (AMP)

"Be careful of the people who come to visit you to make sure you're still stuck. Some people like you better in your brokenness and want to hold you hostage to a lesser version of yourself."

~Pastor John Gray, Relentless Church

Conquering Regrets

"And we know that all things work together for good to those who love God, to those who are the called according to *His* purpose."

Romans 8:28 (NKJV)

Regret as defined in the Merriam-Webster Dictionary, is sadness or disappointment; to mourn the loss of, to miss very much; sorrow aroused by circumstances beyond one's control or power to repair, an expression of distressing emotion.

The above definition is to clarify the difference between 'regret' and the word 'resentment', which I will expand on later in this book. I allowed the spirit of regret to consume my mind and my emotions, as I did with the spirit of fear. From generational job loss to personal relationships I've sabotaged, from losing my virginity as a teenager to low self-esteem and tormenting thoughts of suicide; regrets ran deep once upon a time. Even to the point of guilt, shame, and embarrassment. However, I've learned embarrassment, (guilt and shame) is a choice.

"The steps of a [good and righteous] man are directed *and* established by the Lord, and He delights in his way [and blesses his path]. When he falls, he will not be hurled down, because the Lord is the One who holds his hand *and* sustains him," Psalm 37:23-24 (AMP).

If my Daddy directs my steps, holds my hand, and sustains me, then why would I walk in guilt, shame, or embarrassment of my failures, mistakes and shortcomings? This is not to be confused in any way with taking advantage of God's grace and mercy. We can't keep making unwise choices and think God will ultimately bless and turn a blind eye. There are various consequences to our actions, **Galatians 6:7-8**. However, God's Word clearly explains when we fall (i.e., our mistakes, errors, and shortcomings), it isn't fatal. Every single one is accounted for on our imperfect-journey to our destiny, because God has a grip on our hand and sustains us. Whether we take right or wrong steps, make unwise decisions, even being downright stubborn or naive; our God has made provisions to get us back on track when we've derailed. Truly our God is the Mighty God! This truth is completely unfathomable!

The good news is, through faith and study of the scripture below, I chose to release embarrassment, guilt, and shame of my past and so can you! "***There is*** therefore now no condemnation to those who are in Christ Jesus, who do not walk according to the flesh, but according to the Spirit." Romans 8:1 (NKJV)

Now *as defined in the Merriam-Webster dictionary, is at the present time or moment, in the time immediately before the present, in the time immediately to follow.*

What I've gathered from this definition is that I am consistently, constantly, from one second to the next; from one week to the next; from one year to the next, NEVER, EVER condemned of any sin, failures, or shortcomings; past, present or future. This in itself is truly a miracle through Christ's finished work on the cross. Even if the behaviors of other people are intentionally meant to remind me of my past (often times they are), I am literally free of the sinful nature regardless of how or if they choose to deal with me. It takes my steadfast faith in Christ Jesus and His Word to successfully walk this out daily.

Please understand, those of us who have accepted Jesus as our personal Lord and Savior are the righteousness of God in Christ Jesus; and He loves everyone (saved or unsaved) regardless of how we perform.

33

(2 Corinthians 5:20-21) This revelational truth is in no way a free pass to sin profusely or uncontrollably, as **Romans 6:1** admonishes us to refrain from taking advantage of God's grace to continue sinning. However, we have the confidence in knowing that, when we make a mistake (and we will as we are not perfect), we can get back up and remain forever the righteousness of God in Christ Jesus. And, nothing can reverse that truth. **(Job 29:14, Isaiah 61:10)**

How is this even possible?

The love of God simply cannot be comprehended. Only faith and a daily study of God's Word will keep this incomprehensible reality at the forefront of our minds so we can successfully operate in it. This truth must be embedded into our belief system.

I am now and continually refreshed on this revelation, as I continue to walk out the process, in faith, of having no regrets. My life and steps are ordered by my Father, He delights in my ways and blesses my path. So, I pour out my praise to Immanuel, God with us!

"Brothers and sisters, I do not consider that I have made it my own yet; but one thing *I do*: forgetting what *lies* behind and reaching forward to what *lies* ahead, I press on toward the goal to win the [heavenly] prize of the upward call of God in Christ Jesus."
Philippians 3:13-14 (AMP)

THE PRICE OF THE ANOINTING:

SURRENDERED RESENTMENT

"Do not be overcome and conquered by evil, but overcome evil with good."

Romans 12:21 (AMP)

Resentment as defined by Wikipedia, is a mixture of disappointment, anger and fear. It comprises the three basic emotions of disgust, sadness and surprise-the perception of injustice

Our God is a Complete Gentleman (I like to think of Him as my Gentle Giant). God gave humanity free will, and He will never twist our arm, forcing us to carry out His will. Rather, He will wait you out for when you're ready to become transparent with YOURSELF; for the Father already knows ALL things.

If you are unaware of, or if you choose to ignore the hindrances hidden deep within your being, there are seasons in life where God will get your attention by any means. And, He will surface what's been hiding in darkness, leading you to repentance and then, inevitably, deliverance.

August 2015, in my time with God, I finally became transparent by admitting to Him the resentment I carried for far too long. That day, God opened my eyes and let me see that I'd been carrying streams of resentment toward several others, including myself. God told me that He loved me too much to do me the disservice of allowing me to continue in dysfunction of being gifted and talented, yet undercover and masked. **Romans 8:28** reminded me that ALL things work together for my good because I love God and I'm called according to His purpose.

Check this out

God is so fiercely strategic! He used a generational bloodline curse that plagued me (job loss/job famine) to bring me to the awareness of many other bloodline curses attached to me. During this time at home unemployed, I was able to gain revelation, renounce and dismantle these curses with the Word of God, and begin my journey of putting into action the exact opposite of how these curses came into existence. AND NOW, because of this revelation received, coupled with various action steps taken in faith, every single generational bloodline curse that was attached to me has imploded within each other and out of my life, by faith; thereby catapulting my journey to complete deliverance!!

Did you catch that?

What the enemy meant for evil, God used it for my good, to bring about the outcome of my journey to deliverance, **Genesis 50:20**. Though I experienced loss of employment several times in my life, this very last season of employment famine allotted time for me to become built-up in the Holy Spirit daily, allowing several streams of resentment to be discovered, so I could finally begin my journey to freedom. Freedom to have within me and on me the anointing that would destroy yokes, free the oppressed, set captives free, and heal the brokenhearted **Luke 4:18**, for truly there is an anointing on my life for the ministry of deliverance through dismantling and assassinating generational bloodline curses!

In previous years, these unnecessary streams of resentment were hindering the ministry God placed inside me. For too many years, I was unaware of the burdens buried deep within me, caused by these streams of resentment, that was choking me emotionally, mentally and spiritually.

Interestingly, during that season of brokenness God revealed to me that, at the rate I was going, those hidden streams of resentment would remain undercover and masked, hindering the anointing on my life. Prior to this revelation that brought forth my transformation, I blamed my seasons of employment famine and lack on myself and others. I suggested a list of reasons and explanations for it all, including the reality of it being a generational bloodline curse.

I began to resent my bloodline, wishing God would have connected me to, what I deemed, a better lineage. I had no appreciation for my line of descent whatsoever. I would gaze at other families, assuming the greatness I witnessed of them on the exterior was also just as grand on the interior. And, I was convinced it was a much better deal than what I was connected to. I was angry and even resentful toward God for what He'd connected me to. I began to realize many things in my life were affected by bloodline curses; from continual job loss and relational sabotage, to entertaining the wrong relationships and anxiety from the negative opinions of others; to how my fingers and toes look, and even the spirit of resentment itself; all originating from my bloodline.

BUT GOD!!! In the power of the Holy Spirit, I began to rise above the anxieties I carried regarding my bloodline's dysfunction. I began to rise above being weighed down and emotionally unstable. I began to rise above the negative opinions and the negative outlook on me from others, which once upon a time was mentally and emotionally tormenting. **"but He has said to me, 'My grace is sufficient for you [My lovingkindness and My mercy are more than enough - always available - regardless of the situation]; for [My] power is being perfected [and is completed and shows itself most effectively] in [your] weakness.' 2 Corinthians 12:9 (AMP)**

GOD began to build me up and mature me in His strength and power to withstand all my concerns and anxieties of being connected to my lineage, for there is divine purpose behind my existence, and a greater work. **"It is good for me that I have been afflicted, That I may learn Your statutes." Psalm 119:71 (AMP).**

It all boils down to making the choice and having the patience to allow God the time needed to produce the fruit that He wants in me, in you, and in us. I made the decision to abide in Him and let God's Word abide in me. And, as I daily abide in Him and He in me, every negative stream, every wrong pattern of thinking, every negative stronghold along with the spirit of resentment is forever held captive to the obedience of Christ Jesus **(2 Corinthians 10:5)**!!

WILL YOU HELP ME PUT A LOT OF PRAISE ON THAT? ALL GLORY TO GOD!!!!

Romans 11:29 (NKJV) says, "...the gifts and calling of God are without repentance." Moreover, **Isaiah 10:27** says "...and the yoke shall be destroyed because of the anointing." A songwriter once said, it's the anointing that makes the difference! The Word of God is clear, though my gifts and talents come without repentance, they're of no effect without His anointing!

And now, because of the revelation that brings forth transformation, I have a new appreciation for being connected to my bloodline. My new-found appreciation has very little to do with the 'who or what' of my lineage, rather it has everything to do with my KINGDOM PURPOSE. I am 'assigned' to my bloodline, for such a time as this, to slay every demonic stronghold and crush every curse linked to my family line, freeing myself and my future children, for generations to come!! **Isaiah 61:1-11**

Allow me to share a hard truth that set me all the way free; allow this to free you as well. Although I am purposed and was born for such a dispensation of time as this; even though every generational curse attached to me has been eradicated through the blood of Jesus; in no way is it 'my' responsibility to ensure the previous generations or individuals connected to my bloodline are free. By any means, we are to minister the opportunity of freedom in truth and love as God allows us. Lead them to the water; but we're NOT responsible for their choice on whether or not to drink.

Did you catch that?

The discomforts associated with being connected to the generational curses in my bloodline was tormenting. But I discovered my connection was *not about me* at all. I realized *my comfort* has nothing to do with the purpose for my existence and the greater work God had already begun within me.

My friend, I know I am not alone in what I've experienced regarding hereditary curses. The truth is, so many other bloodline units in the world have some type of dysfunction or another, shared or unshared, quiet as it's kept. But amidst generational bloodline curses and dysfunctions, God WILL ALWAYS raise up at least ONE to break and destroy any and every generational bloodline curse that has controlled that particular unit. And, I'm that ONE!! The buck stops with ME!! And it can stop with YOU too!!

<u>PLEASE UNDERSTAND THIS.</u>

Never believe the lie of the enemy and think you are too educated or above; nor that you're too messed up, beyond repair, or beneath Biblically sound mental health assistance!! And please, do not believe that you're too saved by grace to receive Biblically sound counseling or therapy. Now, please understand, although there's nothing wrong with therapy or counseling, it's not necessarily going to completely resolve your internal issues or struggles. Many (not all) secular counseling platforms are designed to keep you coming back (money focused). And many people seek secular counseling as a means to avoid conforming to the Word of God, which is nothing more than a band-aid on unresolved issues. Ultimately, it's your decision and willingness to conform to the Word of God that will cause you to experience true freedom and victory in your life. However, the misconception that counseling/therapy have no benefits at all has robbed many believers in the Body of Christ and non-believers from becoming mentally healthy. If we didn't need what God has made available to us in the earth, then medical technology would not exist. God will use a variety of avenues as He sees fit to manifest total healing and restoration in your physical, mental, and emotional health. However, it's your willingness to accept and embrace what God says in His Word about YOU. The powerful Word of God and the cleansing blood of Jesus Christ trumps, like none other!

And so, I did myself a favor. I put an end to just attending church out of ritualism and religiosity. I ceased from having a form of Godliness, while my life didn't display the power or presence of the Holy Spirit. I committed to the **never-ever-ending** conformity and transformation power from the Word of God.

I loved and honored myself enough to acquire biblically sound mentors, life coaches, and therapists; and I did my work. One session at a time, I addressed the symptoms and manifestations of the generational bloodline to which I'm connected. I chose to do this for myself, my household, and our children. I did it for the new generational bloodline of the Youngs.

It was my best decision yet!

"Being confident of this very thing, that He who has begun a good work in you will complete it until the day of Jesus Christ." Philippians 1:6 (NKJV)

I AM...ENOUGH!!

"The Lord your God is in your midst,
A Warrior who saves.
He will rejoice over you with joy;
He will be quiet in His love [making no mention
of your past sins], He will rejoice over you
with shouts of joy."

Zephaniah 3:17 (AMP)

The above scripture says it all.

The question is: how can a loving Savior and Lord who is always with us, wins every war, saves us, rejoices over us, and makes no mention of our past sins; not be enough? Who, or what, else are we looking for? Who else can accomplish all that God is?

The answer is simple; humanity is incapable of accomplishing the amazing supernatural truths of Zephaniah 3:17. Prior to committing to God's transformational Word and acquiring therapy/counseling, a portion of the tormenting heaviness I carried in my emotions came via the faces of those whom the enemy suggested would rather not deal with me because of my 'issues'. My main issues consisted of low self-esteem and low self-value, low self-confidence, self-sabotage of friendships, and too many unhealthy friendships due to not knowing my identity in Christ.

My very first experience with the spirit of rejection was encountered at a very young age. As I grew older, I began to realize I didn't know how to be a friend to others. Outside of my mother, the very first friendship I encountered in life failed because of a generational tragedy that occurred within my unit; which was neither my fault, nor the fault of the victim. Even with this tragedy having not been a shared tragic experience of my own, I unknowingly carried its damaging effects into a variety of my relationships.

So, of course the spirit of rejection was accompanied with being overly concerned about people liking and accepting me; the people-pleasing spirit, which is a fruit of the root and dominating spirit of insecurity. The opinions of others mattered way too much to me. With having said this, I can definitely relate to the commonality of the generational bloodline curse of insecurity dominating in today's families. I became secretly devastated and felt like an outcast when I didn't 'fit in' with various circles of people. And to follow of course, would be the spirit of suicide, once the enemy is allowed to convince you that your life is a mistake and you shouldn't have been born. The enemy would whisper, 'Look at the many people who are in harmony with each other; and not you.' And, sadly, these complete lies from the enemy seemed so real; they even seemed to make sense.

I experienced far too many moments throughout my life when all the suggestions and whispers of the enemy caved in on me, sending my emotions 'there' again, and again. 'There' was, once upon a time, an extremely dark and low place of gloom and disappointment I had toward myself regarding the issues I carried.

It was in my last 'there' moment that God spoke to me and gave me the title of this chapter when He asked me, "Aren't I ENOUGH?" The songs that ministered to me during my very last dark experience were "What Love is This" by Kari Jobe and "Why Won't You Let Me Love You" by Ron, Angie & Debbie Winans. In that moment, God wanted me to realize, even if the world is against me, He's more than enough for me **(Romans 8:31)**. In this moment, God invited me to become so filled with His love for me, the overflow would enable me to truly forgive and love others unconditionally and compassionately. How amazing it is to be so filled with God's love that you're able to trust God as you maneuver through life and relationships. God's love can fill you to the point of trusting Him to protect your heart and emotions, even when faced with the possibility of rejection while displaying His love toward another **(Romans 5:5)**.

I'm learning how to become free from the need of an immediate response from others. Sometimes you want people to acknowledge how well you're doing, or to validate your progression, growth and maturity. I acknowledged unto God that HIS approval and validation of me is all that will ever matter, and it will ALWAYS BE ENOUGH! In this moment, I was transparent with God. I admitted to God that it was difficult to focus on His truths when I couldn't see HIS face of approval and validation, because God is in an unseen realm. Instead, all I could see are the faces in the flesh, in the seen realm. A few faces of love, compassion, gentleness; and, yet too many faces of hate, bitterness, dislike, disgust. This was the **perception** with which the enemy attempted to torment me. It literally has taken child-like FAITH for me to believe and rest in God's overall delight and pleasure of ME; and to trust God regarding the hearts of others toward me.

Let's chat about that part: Perception.

It's essential to refrain from making your perception your truth. Our feelings can easily get hurt when we perceive someone has wronged us. Many of my relationships and connections have suffered because I took offense or was overly sensitive. I found that my feelings were frequently hurt, and most people had to walk on eggshells around me. I've constantly felt annoyed or irritated when my expectations from someone in close relationship with me wasn't met. All too frequently, I'd find myself having unnecessary conversations with others or sending text messages, presenting my 'you hurt my feelings' speech. However, I learned the truth, that I do have control over my emotions. I can choose whether to feel offended or not. Just like forgiveness is a choice, not being easily offended is also a choice. Even when we have reason or cause to be offended, Jesus impresses upon our hearts to render kindness, and extend grace **(Ecclesiastes 7:21-22)**. Whether an offense is perceived or intended, it's most imperative to keep the posture of your heart ready to offer and participate in the act of forgiveness, which we will discuss later in <u>What Forgiveness Looks Like</u>.

I truly believe this next scripture is the anthem of the appropriate level of boldness, confidence, self-esteem, and self-value God desires for us to possess. **'I will praise You, for I am fearfully and wonderfully made; Marvelous are Your works, and that my soul knows very well.' Psalm 139:14 (NKJV).** YOU MUST KNOW YOUR WORTH‼ Amidst the faces of your haters, or even those whom the enemy wants us to perceive as haters, we must walk in what I previously mentioned in the <u>Conquering Stigma</u> section of this book. **'Don't let negative treatment from others toward you be the expression of your Heavenly Father.'** My Bishop often teaches, God is NOT mad at us. Please believe, God is not mad at YOU, regardless of any negative outward expression of others!

Regardless of how people treat you, Christians and non-Christians alike, don't believe the lie of the enemy that your Heavenly Father is equally as hateful, disapproving, mad, disgusted, nor bitter toward you as others may be. As I mentioned in the <u>Conquering Stigma</u> section, trust and believe, I know how very challenging it can be to believe God is not mad or disgusted with you when especially a misguided church leader, or someone professing Christ treats you negatively. I understand that you can't see God's face of pleasure and delight in you, amidst the

50

negative faces you can see in the flesh, **(Zephaniah 3:17, Jeremiah 1:8)**. We must activate our FAITH in God's Word; and walk, eat, breathe, sleep God's Word. We must allow God's Word to be a habit, a stronghold in our daily lives. It's the only way to survive the apparent negativity that truly surrounds us on a daily basis. We must walk by faith knowing God is pleased with us, **Psalms 147:11**. Without faith, it's impossible to please God, **Hebrews 11:6**.

An Overwhelming Truth

Exodus 20:4-5 commands us NOT to worship, NOT to bow down, NOT to serve anyone or anything except **God**. Our God is jealous for us!! Our God demands what is rightfully **HIS**. Only God's approval, only God's validation matters!!

Whatever occupies your mind the most becomes your god. The opinions, approvals, and validations of others, when indulged, are developed into idols. When you give too much care and concern regarding what others (positively or negatively) feel and think toward you, in a sense, you are worshipping, bowing down, and serving that which God says he will not have as another god before **HIM!!** When we allow the (negative or positive) opinions of others to consume our minds and our emotions, we now allow this as a distraction to our relationship with God. Flesh left unchecked will do whatever is necessary to be gratified.

And, yes, there are promised consequences for putting another god before our One true and living GOD, should you choose not to repent and turn from it, **Exodus 22:20**. For most of us, it's never our intention to make anything or anyone a god. However, this is the process of how the enemy slow walks us. It becomes an issue within your subconscious mind and, over time, you find yourself completely distracted and overwhelmed with a concern or matter; when you should be overwhelmed with God, His promises, and His truths.

Upon receiving this revelation, I immediately confessed, repented, and received God's forgiveness for 'unknowingly' making the opinions, approval, and validation of others a god!! And, I asked God to assist me in turning from this, as I recognized it was a demonic stronghold needing to be broken and eradicated. NEVER AGAIN will I worship, bow down to, nor serve the opinions of others! Our God is the Provider of every opinion, every approval and every validation we'll ever need. Please understand, it's not that other people's positive opinions and compliments are a bad thing. It's a great thing to esteem another and build each other up.

However, we are expected to look to God for the proper balance, ensuring we don't become prideful within ourselves.

"Anyone who needs other people to approve and validate them has already lost. When you need the approval and validation of people, you will submit to the will of people over the will of God!"

~Pastor John Gray, Relentless Church

Our GOD is enough!!

The only way for God to become enough in your life is through revelation of God's Word. Remember, revelation breeds transformation. "**And do not be conformed to this world [any longer with its superficial values and customs], but be transformed and progressively changed [as you mature spiritually] by the renewing of your mind [focusing on godly values and ethical attitudes], so that you may prove [for yourselves] what the will of God is, that which is good and acceptable and perfect [in His plan and purpose for you].**" Romans 12:2 (AMP).

And, upon renewing your mind and being transformed through the Word of God, you can experience **Philippians 4:7b (TLB)** "**...God's peace, which is far more wonderful than the human mind can understand.**" His peace will keep your thoughts and your hearts quiet and at rest as you trust in Christ Jesus". This will only result in you experiencing **Ephesians 3:19 (NKJV), "to know the love of Christ which passes knowledge; that you may be filled with all the fullness of God."** God's Word is ever-manifesting and true; and it's enough!

In addition to absorbing the Word of God for revelation and transformation, quality time spent with the Holy Spirit is a necessity. **"Draw near to God and He will draw near to you," James 4:8a (NKJV). "For God alone my soul waits in silence; From Him comes my salvation" Psalm 62:1 (AMP).** Life has an interesting way of forcing you to your knees crying out to your Creator, so you might as well discipline yourself and cultivate a prayer life anyway. Become intentional about being in the presence of the Holy Spirit. Become intentional about developing an ever-increasing relationship with the Holy Spirit. The more quality time spent with the Holy Spirit, the clearer you can hear Him speak to your mind and spirit. He will speak to every situation concerning you. Learn to be still, silent, and soak in the presence of the Holy Spirit. He already knows what you have need of; though your long list of needs and desires are not necessary, you can freely present them. The Holy Spirit longs for you to hunger after, thirst after, and

54

chase after His presence!! "O God, You are my God; with deepest longing I will seek You; My soul [my life, my very self] thirsts for You, my flesh longs and sighs for You, In a dry and weary land where there is no water," Psalm 63:1 (AMP). God's overwhelming presence is ever-manifesting and true; and it's enough for you!

Amazing God, your Creator, His breathe in your lungs, your Protector, your Guide, your Warrior; the God that loves you beyond your very comprehension; the God that longs to talk and spend time with you; the God that desires you to long for Him and love Him in return; the God that collects every one of your tears and turns those tears into your victory, for His glory. "Oh! The overwhelming, never-ending, reckless love" of JEHOVAH; THE GREAT I AM. HE IS MORE THAN ENOUGH!!!

"In Your presence is fullness of joy; In Your right hand there are pleasures forevermore," Psalm 16:11b (AMP)

What Forgiveness Looks Like

"And be kind to one another, tenderhearted, forgiving one another, even as God in Christ forgave you."

Ephesians 4:32 (NKJV)

Interestingly, it's impossible to walk out the scripture, above if you haven't *chosen* to be kind to another, haven't *chosen* to be tenderhearted toward another, and haven't *chosen* to forgive another.

Forgive as defined by the Merriam-Webster Dictionary, is to cease to feel resentment against (an offender), to give up resentment of or claim to requital; to grant relief from payment of.

Notice the key action words in the above definition, **cease, give up, grant**. With that said, forgiveness is a *choice.*

Take a moment to absorb that.

It's most vital to understand God's forgiveness of the sins of humanity, the forgiveness human beings should have toward themselves and also for each other.

Once we have been baptized in the name of Jesus Christ for the forgiveness of our sins and received the finished work of Christ on the cross, you must choose to believe the Father has forgiven you. In addition, you must choose to forgive yourself and to forgive others. The same is true with choosing to believe the Father loves you, and also choosing to love yourself and others. If you don't feel forgiven, you'll have a hard time forgiving others. If you typically have a tough time forgiving others, you may not truly feel forgiven yourself.

The forgiveness that God extends to us is conditional based upon our choice to be baptized in the name of Jesus for the forgiveness of our sins, **Acts 2:38**. In addition, confession involves agreeing with God about our sin. If we confess our sins, God has promised to forgive our sins and cleanse us from all unrighteousness, **I John 1:9**.

God has done everything on His part to facilitate forgiveness for us. God is willing to forgive, not wanting anyone to perish, **(2 Peter 3:9)**. Because of Christ's sacrifice on the cross, God freely offers us forgiveness.

God has completely wiped your sin slate clean because of what Jesus Christ did on the cross. All of the things you deserve to be paid back for have been cleared away because God has forgiven you. Ponder how much God has forgiven you, and it'll cause you to be more forgiving of those who have hurt you. Own that statement for yourself, and you'll find it increasingly tough to hold a grudge against someone else. Forgiveness between God and humanity isn't any different from forgiveness among human beings. We forgive out of our love and obedience to God, love of our fellow man, and gratefulness of God's forgiveness toward us through the finished work of the cross. *(Matthew 5:16), (Mark 1:26).* As previously mentioned, forgiveness is choice.

Keep this in mind: No matter what anyone does to you, you'll never have to forgive any other person more than God has already forgiven you. (Let that marinate a moment)

It's important to understand forgiveness does not eliminate all consequences for the offended who may incur mental, emotional or physical hurt, nor the offender who's liable for the damage inflicted. Let's also be clear, this is not a free pass to hold a grudge nor retaliate against someone; nor is God's forgiveness of sin a free pass to habitually hurt others. **Ephesians 4:31, Romans 6:1.**

Undoubtedly, forgiveness jumpstarts the necessary process or journey to becoming completely healed of the hurt incurred after a suffered wrong. Depending on the nature and the severity of an offense, emotional, mental and physical wounds may still need to be healed, as we are human. However, after having forgiven, you may walk away still hurt, damaged, and scarred. And, this is where many people grow bitter and angry over time, because the actual hurt has not been properly dealt with. Upon our willingness to follow through with the biblical requirement of forgiveness, we all too often negate the necessary repair of damages caused by some offenses.

The popular cliché is, "Time heals all wounds." I believe in 'time', however, time spent doing nothing besides waiting for your wounds to somehow disappear is a common mistake. You mustn't sit in any level of pain, and allow it to grow like mold untreated, as you will be left to rot. Hence, leaving a stench that will begin to invade and irritate your mind, emotions, and your relationships at large, including your relationship with Christ. Rather, invest time in God's Word regarding your hurt, time in God's presence about your pain, time with a church leader, a biblically sound counselor, therapist, or life coach regarding your mental and emotional health. The same time most of us would take to see a physician for the pain or ailments in our physical bodies is the same time that should be taken for healing from emotional and mental damage. This time of healing and restoration for yourself must be priority.

Forgiveness is the solitary act of an individual heart, since it's a direct command from God to an individual. Forgiveness is only about what happens within the offended person's heart; it's not contingent on another person, rather it's about the offended person's preservation. Forgiveness allows an offended individual to be free and released from what others may have said or done, whether the offense has been acknowledged or not. **"Take heed to yourselves. If your brother sins against you, rebuke him; and if he repents, forgive him." Luke 17:3 (NKJV).**

Forgiveness is a decision, a deliberate choice, not an emotion or feeling. Your feelings may or may not accompany forgiveness. Feelings of bitterness against a person can fade with time in the Word of God and time spent with the Holy Spirit; or even biblically sound therapy or counseling. In our relationships, we'll often need to choose to have a right attitude and render forgiveness BEFORE our wounded heart has healed. **Forgiveness is not about being set free from feelings, rather from the** person and the offense said and/or done against you. *Therein lies your freedom.*

I challenge you to take a moment and think about this.

We must extend forgiveness to those who don't deserve it. There are numerous examples that charge us to forgive others, even when they don't deserve it, **Acts 7: 59-60**. I think about Jesus on the cross in the midst of his executioners: **"Father, forgive them, for they know not what they do" Luke 23:34 (NKJV)**. Also, **John 13** where Jesus knew Judas would betray him. When I find myself having trouble extending forgiveness to someone I've deemed undeserving, I reflect on how unworthy I am of God's forgiveness. Yet, He sees fit to continue loving and forgiving me. When considering the magnitude of that, withholding forgiveness from others who've hurt me seems trivial.

We must extend forgiveness to others even when they don't ask for it. **"If a brother sins against you, go to him privately and confront him with his fault. If he listens and confesses it, you have won back a brother, Matthew 18: 15 (AMP)**. When we are wronged by someone, we naturally expect them to come to us and say, "I apologize." Yes, *that is the right thing to do*, however, God commands us to be the *initiators* in the forgiveness transaction. We should go to our brother or sister and respectfully and lovingly talk it out. It's not an easy thing to do; it's down right inconvenient and feels unfair, but it's a critical act in being able to move forward in relationship with God and others.

We must extend an unlimited amount of forgiveness to others. **"Then Peter came to him and asked, "Sir, how often should I forgive a brother who sins against me? Seven times?" "No!" Jesus replied, "seventy times seven! Matthew 18: 21-22 (TLB).** Forgiving seems difficult, and repeating it over and over again can seem impossible. But, with God, all things are possible, **Matthew 19:26**. Jesus is clear in this passage that there is no "final straw" that warrants us withholding our forgiveness. God doesn't have a "final straw" for us. To be clear, this doesn't mean allowing others to take advantage of your forgiveness (I'll briefly discuss the trust factor later in this section). God also gave us the ability to be reasonable and make smart choices with our lives. However, holding on to unforgiveness and resentment only takes our joy, while doing no harm to the other party. We should forgive repeatedly because *God commands it...period.*

Forbearance is a product of God's love, which initiates true forgiveness, **Galatians 5:22-23**. We can determine how we act and what we do with how we feel. To forbear, as defined by Google, is patient self-control; restraint and tolerance. As it relates to an offense, we should patiently restrain an impulse to negatively respond or react and maintain self-control in the face of frustration, where a suffered wrong has not been resolved. Forbearance causes us to weigh a suffered wrong or offense with love, wisdom, discernment, and God's Word; and *choose* not to respond negatively. Scripture uses various words for this quality: patience, longsuffering, endurance, and forbearance, **(Proverbs 12:16, 19:11; 1 Peter 4:8, Galatians 5:22)**.

Forgiveness is NOT the automatic restoration of trust.

For instance, assuming that forgiving a physically abusive spouse means the need for separation should end immediately as well isn't wise, nor is it required. Scripture gives us many reasons to distrust those who have proven themselves untrustworthy **(Luke 16:10-12)**. Rebuilding trust can only begin after true forgiveness, and the process of reconciliation which, of course, involves confession and repentance. Notice I said "rebuilding" because trust is not automatic, it's a process!

Ephesians 4:31 is very clear, harboring bitterness in our hearts is **sin**. And, if we aren't actively seeking to kill it, it will break our fellowship with God. Ultimately, we won't experience everything God has to offer us. While we must not repay evil for evil **(1 Peter 3:9)**, nor harbor bitterness in our hearts **(Hebrews 12:15)**, forgiveness is required, and should be made available from everyone, to everyone. We all should maintain an attitude of readiness, with our hearts postured to forgive. **Matthew 5: 23-24**.

I discovered part of why I'd been emotionally weighty, and why it seemed offenses between me and another were smoothed over, but not properly dealt with. It's because the 'proper' way to deal with offenses is to *choose* to automatically forgive another, *requiring nothing more from them*, as God in Christ Jesus has forgiven me, requiring nothing of me than to receive His forgiveness. Forgiveness is a biblical requirement, all too often not practiced.

Reconciliation, as defined by Cambridge Dictionary, is a situation in which two people or groups of people become friendly again after they have argued: the process of making two opposite beliefs, ideas, or situations agree.

Matthew 5:24 admonishes us to work things out between each other and make things right, before we offer worship to God, and then come back to offer our gift of worship unto God. Our God has has already facilitated the ministry of reconciliation, made available to us through Jesus Christ our Lord, **2 Corinthians 5:18**.

While forgiveness involves us releasing another from their offense, reconciliation involves acknowledging and owning up to that offense, toward another. We all must come to the table of reconciliation, having forgiven each other in advance, otherwise reconciliation will not occur. True reconciliation involves sincere, heartfelt repentance (apology), in order for relationship to be restored.

Sadly, even with the sincerest efforts for peace and reconciliation, I would sometimes participate in unresolved issues being 'pushed under the rug' as to avoid being stigmatized as being the 'drama queen' or 'trouble maker.' Let's just be honest, some of us would rather not go through the tunnel of chaos, and we sometimes avoid the healthy and necessary confrontation to bring resolve and reconciliation to a negative situation, because confrontation exposes our contribution to an issue on the table. Some of us would have to own our mess, shortcomings and imperfections; and most of us detest that, because it's downright uncomfortable to have to admit where we went wrong, and render an apology during the process of reconciliation. Isn't it?

My, my, my. It's OK to say 'OUCH', trust me I've had to swallow this horse pill as well.

So, let's review the aforementioned. God is ready to forgive, however we must also be ready to forgive others. God stands ready and willing to forgive us, but REQUIRES that we extend the same forgiveness to others as well. **Matthew 6:14-25** can be a difficult scripture to process. Although our feelings and emotions are valid, obedience to the Word of God is crucial. If we have resentment and bitterness in our hearts, it's time to surrender it over to God; let Him heal us and enable us to forgive others. Do not base forgiveness on how you feel. Make the choice to obey. Our destiny is dependent on it.

I'm so overwhelmingly grateful to God for this revelation. Because of the finished work of the cross, I have forgiven myself and others; because God thought it not robbery to forgive me!!

"Confess your trespasses to one another, and pray for one another, that you may be healed. The effective, fervent prayer of a righteous man avails much." James 5:16 (NKJV)

WHAT CONQUERING LOOKS LIKE

I will let everyone who conquers sit beside me on my throne, just as I took my place with my Father on his throne when I had conquered.

Revelation 3:21 (TLB)

Conquer as defined by the Merriam-Webster Dictionary, is to gain, acquire or overcome by force of arms; to gain mastery over or win by overcoming obstacles or opposition; to overcome by mental or moral power.

This book's foundational scripture reassures us in Romans 8:37, in all these things, we are more than conquerors. What exactly are *all these things* this scripture is referring to? **Romans 8:37-39, Message Bible** in particular refers to all these things as trouble, hard times, hatred, hunger, homelessness, bullying threats, backstabbing, and even the worst sins listed in scripture. And we know the list of sins and life circumstances is much longer than this!

Yet we are *more than conquerors*!!

In the Kingdom of God, to conquer is to be victorious in adversity. To be "more than a conqueror" means we not only achieve victory, but we are *overwhelmingly* victorious! **"No weapon that is formed against you will succeed; And every tongue that rises against you in judgment you will condemn. This [peace, righteousness, security, and triumph over opposition] is the heritage of the servants of the Lord, And *this is* their vindication from Me," says the Lord, Isaiah 54:17 (AMP).** We know that our opposition (satan) will put up a fight, but he's no match for the victors (Kingdom Citizens of God). Our win is well beyond the scope of a mundane victory!

<u>In Times Of A Set Back Or A 'Dumb Day'</u>

Please understand, conquering is in *no way to be confused* with having "arrived" in terms of perfection or having it all together. As long as you are alive on this earth, YOU WILL fall short, make mistakes and as my Bishop would say have 'dumb days', **Romans 7:14-25**. Further, **Romans 3:23 (AMP) since all have sinned and continually fall short of the glory of God.** Notice in the last scripture the word 'continually.' It's truly inevitable and there's just no way around being imperfect. God allows our imperfections to manifest, so we are just that more aware of how desperately we need HIM, for we can do nothing without HIM, **John 15:5**.

A conqueror understands spiritual growth is a necessary part of a believer's life; accepts the process will take time and does not seek quick fixes, rather focuses on the long term progression. In no way are we as imperfect creations given a pass to sin profusely, **Romans 6:1-23**. However, The enemy tries to deceive and even torment us with evil suggestions that we are just not good enough, will never get it right, will always be this way; and we in turn place unnecessary pressure and unrealistic expectations on ourselves. WE ARE 'human' Kingdom Citizens, and our God is fully aware.

A conqueror avoids temptations that weaken their ability to overcome by setting defenses and boundaries. A conqueror speaks honestly about their spiritual battles; while proactively informing others (designated accountability/support partners) of temptations or high risk situations they are facing; humbly submitting to wise counsel, even during times of victory over temptation. If there is a set back or a 'dumb day', a conqueror confesses sin soon after it occurs **Psalm 32:3-5, James 5:16**.

A conqueror believes wholeheartedly in God's forgiveness and does not take it for granted; rather their heart is toward God as they strive for obedience to God's Word, **Revelation 14:12**. A conqueror believes in the critical need for grace, humbly repents, receives God's forgiveness and **moves forward** *Philippians 3:13*.

With that said, **never allow anyone** of any status, title or position; relatives, those at church nor in the workplace to shut you down, and disqualify your deliverance process from any struggle, just because you may have a 'dumb day'. As stated in the preface of this book, I am still on the potter's wheel...***daily***. I've not arrived because I've written this book; rather even while in the 'process' and on my imperfect-progressive journey, my *decision* to be a conqueror coupled with God's grace actually qualifies me as More Than A Conqueror! And *YOUR decision* to be a conqueror, starting today, makes you eligible as being More Than A Conqueror as well! How's that for God's miraculous truth!

But thanks be to God, who gives us the victory [as conquerors] through our Lord Jesus Christ. 1 Corinthians 15:57 (AMP)

COMPASSION FOR THE UNCOMPASSIONATE

"Since you have been chosen by God who has given you this new kind of life, and because of his deep love and concern for you, you should practice tenderhearted mercy and kindness to others. Don't worry about making a good impression on them, but be ready to suffer quietly and patiently."

Colossians 3:12 (TLB)

Compassion as defined in the Merriam-Webster Dictionary is the sympathetic consciousness of others' distress together with a desire to alleviate it.

As with forgiveness, to the degree I desire others to be lovingly compassionate toward me, is to the same degree I must be lovingly compassionate toward others, **(Luke 6:31)**. This includes "self-compassion," which speaks to and supports the Conquering Regrets section of this book.

Self-compassion as defined by Wikipedia, is extending kindness to oneself in instances of perceived inadequacy, shortcomings, or general pain and suffering; rather than ignoring them or hurting oneself with self-criticism.

Aside from the process of unconcern for how others view me, I believe the hardest thing I've had to face, in my life, is demonstrating loving compassion toward myself. And, demonstrating that same compassion to those who lack compassion for myself, and others. Through my experiences of rejection from others and even myself and, wrongfully accepting the stigma attached to my name; I've discovered only individuals in a deep-rooted relationship with Christ can accomplish this. Receiving the loving compassion of Christ by faith, allows me to demonstrate loving compassion toward myself and others. This is the key to maintaining my deliverance.

Rejection from others can be hurtful. It has been for me and I'm certain you can attest to the same. After all, we are human and naturally desire to be loved and accepted. God created us to desire and give love. However, as my Bishop often teaches, **"the opinions and acceptance of others only matters to the degree that you need them."** This teaching and enlightenment made it possible and easier for me to demonstrate the compassion of Christ toward others, especially those who rejected and stigmatized me. It's so much easier to demonstrate the compassion of Christ toward individuals that reciprocate it, or those who are just easy to love and get along with. Of course, that's all too easy. But we're not called to partake in the easy stuff only. **"But if you love those who love you, what credit is that to you? For even sinners love those who love them." Luke 6:32 (NKJV)**

True ministry is the demonstration of the compassion of Christ, particularly toward individuals that give you their back and want nothing to do with you. Folks who have labeled you or have a negative opinion or view of you; haters in general. And, these I speak of (in my many years of experiencing stigma and rejection) are often misguided Christians. A few of my former pastors, ministers, leaders, some relatives and former friends have fallen in this category. Not all, but many of the aforementioned proclaim the love of Christ in their hearts; yet have demonstrated toward me quite the opposite. If one is already hurting, the last thing the person needs is for those who claim to have the love and compassion of Christ to kick them while they're down.

Here's a revelation God downloaded to me. Although we all should absolutely demonstrate compassion toward each other as the Word of God instructs us, many will not and sadly cannot. Many of us lack the Word and do not operate as the Word of God instructs. Therefore, it's equally important to practice being in the presence of the Holy Spirit and absorbing the Word of God; as to guard our hearts from the extremely high probability of encountering uncompassionate personalities.

Prior to this revelation, my expectation was the exact opposite, especially that of blood-washed believers which made my encounters with the uncompassionate that more painful. Many uncompassionate people we'll come across do not know the first thing about what to do with our 'issues and shortcomings'. A high expectation of compassion from another toward you can have its downfalls. In general, people can't fulfill you in any area. Only God is designed to fulfill and complete you. Some of us are angry at people because they're not giving us what we think we need, but only God can give you what you need.

Disappointment and devastation can result from the expectation in others to demonstrate compassion toward you. From your family unit, to your friends, to the boss on your job and ministry leaders at church; it's important to understand that even those whom you value greatly or hold in high esteem are capable of lacking compassion. I've learned through many of my previous experiences shared in this book, it should not be assumed a person's title, position or status deems them capable of demonstrating compassion.

Regardless of titles, positions or status, many people may not possess within themselves God's Word nor His love; therefore, they don't know what, why, how or when to speak to and pour in you who God says you are. Many choose not to see you from God's perspective, since your brokenness may be more comfortable and convenient for them.

I hope you caught that...

Many uncompassionate people are hurting and unresolved deep within themselves from their own compassion-deficient experiences. Hurt people hurt people. Therefore, some individuals choose to magnify your issues or shortcomings, which is an 'unhealthy' coping mechanism for them; deflecting their own insecurities, struggles and brokenness. Make no mistake, this goes for even the most anointed, most successful, most esteemed people with significant titles, positions, and status.

"The length a person will go to in order to prove a point, paints a pretty vivid picture of the level of their struggle and insecurities."

~Shannon White, Reignite Coaching Solutions

I use the word demonstrate quite often in this chapter to help you understand that compassionate Christ-like love involves action. It's not just a feeling or a thought. We may never have known the love Christ has for us had it not been for the demonstration of His love on the cross at Calvary, **Romans 5:6**. As Christians made in Christ's image (**Genesis 1:27,9:6**), we are to demonstrate His love and compassion by dying to ourselves **Luke 9:23**, despite the hurt or unfairness we may experience day to day; just as He did when He walked the earth.

I've discovered two things that make demonstrating the compassionate love of Christ easier. The first is understanding how much God loved me in spite of me, **Ephesians 2:4-5**. When we take the time to reflect on how much of a ratchet mess we've all been, and can still be at times, we gain more of an understanding of God's mercy and grace. How can reflecting on what we could have been, if not for God's unconditional love, not humble our hearts? Once our hearts have been humbled by this awareness, how can we not demonstrate the love and compassion of Christ toward others?

The second is understanding how much God loves the individual towards whom you find difficulty demonstrating His love; in the same way God demonstrates His love towards a difficult, rough-around-the-edges, ratchet YOU, **John 13:34**. It's imperative to remember God's incomprehensible love. Often, it's easy to remember God's love while waters are calm and peaceful. However, when various relational conflicts and storms surface (and they will), this is when the demonstration of God's love and compassion counts the most.

As previously mentioned in the <u>What Forgiveness Looks Like</u> section of this book, forgiveness is a commitment to pardon the offender from the offense. That means, you never rehearse the offense, you never remind the offender, nor others about the offense. With that said, forgiveness surrenders the right to retaliate.

Retaliation as defined in Vocabulary.com is an act of revenge.

Many people often confuse and limit retaliation to repaying the offender to the exact measure or degree he or she is offended. Retaliation has many faces, many actions, and many words. Some may not go to the extremity of mirroring the very offense they received, claiming to have obeyed the Word of God **(Romans 12:17)**. Rather, they will render a negative attitude or disposition, negative silence or negative distance or avoidance, which are all still deemed retaliation. Many of us even vent (defined as gossip) to a confidant, or even slander, with intent to portray their offender as the 'sinner' when in fact, this behavior is sin itself. This to include, but is not limited to i.e., negative social media posts that insinuate details of conflict that have just occurred between you and your offender; displaying your negative feelings about it, thereby wrongfully exposing your offender.

Exposing your offender and announcing the details of their offense is not your job. It's so imperative to understand, and remain in your lane, versus God's lane. **"Repay no one evil for evil. Have regard for good things in the sight of all men. If it is possible, as much as depends on you, live peaceably with all men. Beloved, do not avenge yourselves, but rather give place to wrath; for it is written, 'Vengeance is Mine, I will repay,' says the Lord." Romans 12: 17-19 (NKJV).** And even when God deals justly with your offender, as we can expect He will, we are still to remain in our lane, administer and demonstrate the love and compassion of the Father. **"Do not rejoice** *and* **gloat when your enemy falls, And do not let your heart be glad [in self-righteousness] when he stumbles,"** Proverbs 24:17 (AMP).

"Thus has the Lord of hosts said, 'Dispense true justice and practice kindness and compassion, to each other;" Zechariah 7:9 (AMP).

In summary, obeying God's commands to forgive and demonstrate His love and compassion toward others may seem like others are winning and you're losing. Of course, that's the wrong perspective the enemy is hoping you'll accept and sit in; but don't. Please do not mistake that misconception with God being unconcerned about how you feel, as your feelings are valid and you are His beloved. The rewarding truth is, when we yield to the demonstration of compassion, we'll discover it's accompanied by a level of pity, sympathy and understanding regarding another's negative behavior; which in turn, has the ability to ultimately minimize and even dismiss inner frustrations within ourselves. Therefore, the need to retaliate or repay another for an offense said or done against us is trivial, hence this revelation, coupled with God's promise in **Zechariah 7:9**. This is not to be confused in any way with tolerating any level of abuse or injustice, should another choose to continue in their dysfunction which is negatively impacting your space or your life. Our God NEVER expects us to be anyone's doormat in the name of compassion and pity; rather it is very possible to honor our God, His Word and ourselves simultaneously and in proper balance. It's called 'healthy relational boundaries.'

My friend, be encouraged and know every offense, every hurt, every wound, every scar, damaged emotions, mental strongholds and all, WILL BE eradicated by the powerful blood of Jesus, when we surrender our brokenness to Him! "If your heart is broken, you'll find God right there; if you're kicked in the gut, he'll help you catch your breath." Psalm 34:18 (MSG). Our God is our great defender and vindicator. It's so much better His way. His glory, your victory!! (Psalm 18).

"The Rock! His work is perfect, For all His ways are just; A God of faithfulness without iniquity (injustice), Just and upright is He." Deuteronomy 32:4 (AMP)

NOT YOUR LIFE...

"And they overcame and conquered him because of the blood of the Lamb and because of the word of their testimony, for they did not love their life and renounce their faith even when faced with death."

Revelation 12:11 (AMP)

We can overcome the accuser (satan) by the testimony the Holy Spirit will create in us if we are willing and obedient. No matter how ugly or uncomfortable the essence of overcoming and conquering the enemy is, stand confidently and boldly in God, and in your truth, for the saving of many lives. When we learn to focus on God's purpose, we see the true purpose for our existence.

"If you don't go all the way with me, through thick and thin, you don't deserve me. If your first concern is to look after yourself, you'll never find yourself. But if you forget about yourself and look to me, you'll find both yourself and me," Matthew 10:38-39 (MSG).

Loving your life not unto death also involves being unconcerned about the views and opinions of others about your life. Becoming

82

attached to the temporal things of this world that we see in the natural is evidence we're too attached to our life or our soul and its carnal desires. That doesn't just pertain to material and tangible things, but also people, people's opinions, approval, and validation of you, which is void of importance. How can it be, when God declares WHO and WHAT YOU ARE? Being concerned with how others will view you after sharing your testimony and exposing truth is equivalent to idolizing, as shared in the I Am...Enough!! section of this book. Our jealous God will not accept us being attached and overly concerned about anything or anyone above Him! **(Exodus 20:3-5).**

Revelation 12:11b deals with dying to yourself, forfeiting your comfortability, and not being so in love and protective of yourself, reputation, and status that you're unwilling to share your story with others. Most of us may not become martyrs, but by putting aside comfort, laying down pride, and dying to our flesh altogether; we can follow the example of Christ by demonstrating sacrificially through our shared testimonies. Not loving our own lives means putting God and others before ourselves.

Since when are our lives on earth about fulfilling our own desires and needs? We must humble ourselves before our almighty

God. Our lives are not our own, we belong to God. Let's not forget we were bought with a price, (1 Corinthians 6:19-20). "For you died [to this world], and your [new, real] life is hidden with Christ in God." Colossians 3:3 (AMP). And, only God can choose our path (Jeremiah 10:23).

So many need to hear the testimonies of those who've experienced or are still experiencing the same struggle or trial they are. Shared testimonies are like medical referrals. It's your experience of a particular trial and the victory won through Christ that compels others to give Dr. Jesus a try. And we all know, when you get great service from a great doctor you're more prone to tell everyone that you've hit the jackpot with that great doctor! So, it is with our great God. How can we keep quiet and not share everything our God has done with those in need of victory? **Come and hear, all who fear God [and worship Him with awe-inspired reverence and obedience], And I will tell what He has done for me. Psalm 66:16 (AMP).**

I encourage you to reflect on the testimonies I've shared in this book, and of those you've encountered from others previously. I challenge you to seek the Holy Spirit on how He's calling you to share your testimony sacrificially, for the saving of many lives.

"For whoever wishes to save his life [in this world] will [eventually] lose it [through death], but whoever loses his life [in this world] for My sake will find it [that is, life with Me for all eternity]." Matthew 16:25 (AMP)

PRAYER TO BREAK GENERATIONAL BLOODLINE CURSES

Our children, and our children's children, will not know about the goodness of God's Spirit if we surround them with dark spirits. If we sow bad seed then we are feeding our children bad fruit. If we live wrong, we teach our children to live wrong. If we bring curses upon ourselves, then we bring those same curses upon to our children. If we bring cursed things into our home, then we are surrounding our children with cursed things, accustoming them to the ways of this world. If we are becoming familiar with dark spirits by living wrong then we are introducing our children to dark spirits and making these spirits familiar to them.

Let's Pray in the Spirit of Warfare...

Jesus Christ I confess and I proclaim that You are Savior and Lord over my life. I proclaim that the stripes You bore on the Cross at Calvary have established You as "my Redeemer." You are my Master, my Shepherd, my Healer and my Deliverer. I proclaim that Jehovah, Creator of the heavens and the earth, is my God and my Spiritual Father in whom I trust, and in who I am trusting upon this day to set me free from the *"iniquities of my fathers,"* from *'past un-godly vows that may have been spoken over my family'* and from the *'generational curses caused by these iniquities'* which have been traveling through my ancestral bloodlines.

In the name of Jesus Christ, I declare that I am not in agreement to any form of *sin,* or *disobedience* that operates in this world and against the throne of God, as I am not in agreement to any person, or family member who deliberately sins, or perverts God's ways. In the Mighty name of Jesus Christ I praise You Father God for Your good and righteous ways and I seek to live by Your Spirit and reap the rewards of living by Your righteousness.

I repent for every **relative connected to my family ancestry** who has **deliberately,** or **without spiritual wisdom** sinned against my God, Jehovah, or His people. I realize that all sin will be judged one day and that each one of us is accountable for what we have said, or done, but I am repenting for the sins of my bloodline, so that I shall be released from any curse these sins may have produced against me. I atone for every family member from my heritage who has entered onto sinful paths and who has opened doors

never before opened giving Satan greater influence over **their** lives and the lives of their **children.**

I intercede the Blood of Jesus Christ for those members in my bloodline who had a good heart, but sinned because they were blinded by ignorance. Have mercy on them Father God and forgive their ignorance.

I renounce the behavior of any relative in our bloodline who has lived more for the world, than for God. I renounce any ungodly beliefs, traditions, rituals, or customs my people may have followed. I repent of those in my bloodline who sought to fulfill the selfishness of their desires, and those who have perverted God's righteousness; for I myself choose to serve God and live by His ways.

In the name of Jesus Christ, I declare Father God, You will sever from me and redeem me of every oppressing sinful influence that has found a way into my life because of a deliberate sin I have committed, for I repent of them, and I declare Father in Jesus Christ's name that every **'sin of the fathers'** as stated in **Exodus 20:4-6 (NKJV)** that operates against me will be nullified in the name of Jesus Christ and broken off of me and my children, for I repent of these also. In Jesus' name, Amen!

RIGHT NOW... *If there is anything you feel led to renounce regarding your bloodline, or its heritage, do so now!! Renounce it out of your family, renounce it out of your marriage, out of your household, out of your finances, out of your physical body and your health, out of your mind, out of your emotions, out of your heart...in the NAME OF JESUS!!!*

Let's Declare...

By my authority in *Jesus Christ* I command every violation of *"bloodline iniquity"* perpetrated in my family going back four generations to be **uprooted** from my family and I command it's work, of oppression and curses to be **broken from me and my children** this moment!

I declare these curses null and void in Jesus Christ's name. By the atoning Blood of Jesus Christ, I take charge over these sins, curses, and spirits responsible for enforcing these curses and I command them to go to dry and arid places, back to the pit of hell. In the name of Jesus Christ, I also take charge over every **ungodly** "vow or oath" spoken over, or against my family (whether by a family member, friend or a stranger) to be covered over by the Blood of Jesus Christ and declared null and void in Jesus Christ's name!!

I am a child of the King bought and paid for by the Blood of Jesus Christ and I command every generational curse and their manifestations of sicknesses, dysfunctional lifestyles, failed marriages, character flaws, financial poverty, spiritual oppression, or any other manifested curse against my family to be broken off of me and my family now in Jesus Christ's name!!

I intercede the Blood of Jesus Christ, and I command the roots of these curses that have engrafted themselves against me to be uprooted and destroyed in the same way that Jesus had spoken words against the fig tree in **Matthew 21:19-21 (NKJV)** and that tree withered up and died.

DECLARE THIS WITH AUTHORITY: Let these curses die now!! I cancel any assignments of revenge and retaliation that seek to wreak havoc as a counter attack against me, my family and anyone connected to me!! Authority over Satan's darkness is ours in Jesus Christ, and Jesus has given us this Authority, and I claim this authority. *Luke 10:19* **(NKJV)**. In the name of Jesus Christ. *"Amen"*

Give God Your Praises & All Of The Glory!

Booking Information

Want *AYoungLady*, at your next ministry event?

I'm available for speaking engagements, panel discussions, and other events that empower men and women to not just *Imagine*, but *Conquer* generational bloodline curses.

email ayounglady07@gmail.com or call 856.353.8272

Made in the USA
Middletown, DE
17 August 2019